The Lord will Make a Way

Pastor Janis Barnes

No part of this publication may be reproduced, stored, or transmitted in
any form or by any means, electronic, mechanical, photocopying,
recording, scanning, or otherwise, except as permitted under Section 107
or 108 of the 1976 United States Copyright Act without the prior written
permission of the author. Requests to the author or publisher for permission should be addressed to the following email:JanisBarnes28@gmail.com
 Limit of liability/disclaimer of warranty: While the
publisher and author have used their best efforts in preparing this guide,
they make no representation or warranties with respect to the accuracy or
completeness of the contents of this document and specifically disclaim
any implied warranties of merchantability or fitness for particular purpose.
No warranty may be created or extended by sales representatives,
promoters, or written sales materials.
The advice and strategies contained herein may not be suitable for your
situation. You should consult with a professional where appropriate.
Neither the publisher nor the author shall be liable for any loss of profit or
any other commercial damages, including but not limited to special,
incidental, consequential, or other damages.

Copyright© 2020

Acknowledgements

Thanks To:

My mother Reverend Martina Dorothy Thomas-Madden who always shared the history of our family. I learned that my grandmother Mable Thomas always said, "The Lord will make a way somehow!" Through you as a widow, single parent, I saw the Lord make a way! For my children Eugene III, Jordan, Jasmine, and Ian. Through you, as your mother, I learned The Lord Will Make a Way!

First Lady Arnette Stewart, you were the one who took my emails and printed them and gave them to me in book form as a gift. God used you to tell me it's time to write and publish my book.

Sparkle Smith thank you for being patient with me and mentoring me in the book editing and publishing process.

Cheryl Polote-Williamson my Sorority Sister, Mentor and Friend. Thank you for inspiring me, supporting me and sharing with me so many things about writing your vision. Getting this book published is a manifestation of what I wrote at one of your Vision Board Workshops!

To my family, friends, mentors and the many people in my life who have supported, challenged and prayed for me; it would take another book to name you all! If our paths have crossed, yes, I thank you!

Table of Contents

Email 1: Peace in The Midst of Trial

Email 2: Are you Walking in Your Calling?

Email 3: Only What you do for Christ Will Last!

Email 4: God Is Protecting You!

Email 5: God Knows Me

Email 6: All My Hope is in the Lord

Email 7: Be Not Afraid, Only Believe

Email 8: Rejoice

Email 9: God's Plan

Email 10: Bless You

Email 11: God's Favor

Email 12: Take your Burdens to the Lord and Leave them there.

Email 13: Lord Help Me Do The Work

Email 14: Where's The Fruit

Table of Contents Continued

Email 15: It's Possible

Email 16: Your Joy

Email 17: God will lift You.

Email 18: Wonderful Revelations

Email 19: The Lord is Faithful

Email 20: Grace and Peace

Email 21: My Shelter

Email 22: Praise God for Your Victory

Email 23: God Has Not Forgotten You

Email 24: What Will God Require?
Email 25: Don't Worry God Will Provide

Email 26: Positive Attitude

Email 27: The Truth

Email 28: No Greater Love

Email 29: Man meant it for evil, But God meant it for your Good

Email 30: No one can stop God's Plan For you!

Email 31: I know the Lord for Myself

Email 32: I'm So Glad God's Ways Are Not our Ways

Email 33: Believe!

Email 34: A Treasure in My Heart

Email 35: You Don't Have to Worry

Email 36: If it had not been for the Lord who was on my side Where Would I Be?

Email 37: The Pursuit of Happiness

Email 38: Radical Praise

Email 39: Trust in The Lord!

Introduction

Years ago, I would send each morning, an encouraging inspiring and uplifting group email. I would also share the email content on social media. God would give me the right words and scriptures to share. Every morning email was exactly what the group needed to hear at the exact time it was sent. It was like a tailor-made word from heaven. The daily group emails had a standard theme. I titled each daily expected email "***The Lord Will Make a Way***". I was inspired by my grandmother, a mother of eleven children who at times was not sure how she was going to feed her family but never had to eat leftovers! Her phrase of saying, **"The Lord Will Make a Way"**, is a confirmation of the providence of God in my grandmother's life and a result of her enduring, persevering, and monumental faith. That faith was passed down to my mother and was then passed down to me. I trust that as you begin this devotion, you begin to remember the ways He has made and the doors He has opened for you. I also trust this devotion will provide you with insight on how He will continue to make a way. I hope you begin to understand your position along the journey as He continues to make a way for you. So, let's begin the journey. Buckle your seatbelts!

Email 1:

Peace in the midst of trial.

Thou preparest a table before me in the presence of mine enemies. Mine cup runneth over. Psalm 23:5 KJV

Good Morning!

I'm sure you have experienced many hardships, however, what can you give thanks for in the midst of the trials you are currently experiencing?

Have a Great Day!

Rev Janis Barnes

1. Can you name at least two blessings you have in the midst of the trials you are experiencing?

2. How has your faith remained charged because of the blessings that you currently have?

3. How well can being mature enough to handle the blessings prepare you for the table set before you?

4. Why do you believe some people think that peace is more priceless than fortune?

Email 2

Are you walking in your calling"?

Focus on how God blesses us and our situation for our lives. God has revealed many things to us, but we have not focused on what He has revealed, and in the process, we lost the perspective He wanted us to focus on.

Be strong and courageous. Do not be afraid or terrified because the Lord God goes with you, and He will never leave you nor forsake you NIV Deuteronomy 31:6

Good Morning!

Wherever you go He will be there. Keep His presence near and you do not have to be afraid, and He has afforded you courage and strength, so you do not have to settle in weariness because strength is a promise to you.

Have a Great Day!

Rev Janis Barnes

1. Has God spoken to you about your calling? Are you answering that call? If not, which voices are calling you so that you are not answering? Is it your job? Career? Business? Home? Family? Friends, etc. or what others think?

2. Is self -condemnation preventing you from your calling? If so, take a moment to focus on the greatness inside of you.

3. What greatness on the inside of you has God revealed to you?

4. How will you allow God to use the greatness on the inside of you as a springboard to your calling?

Email 3

Only what you do for Christ will last!

And whatsoever ye do, do it heartily, as to the Lord, and not unto men; (Colossians 3:23 KJV)

Good Day!

Many people are motivated in life to do things to receive self-gratification. On the job when some people try to get noticed they say and do things that are kind to the boss. Not because they are sincere, but because they want to get ahead.

We see in Colossians 3:23, to paraphrase only what we do for Christ will last! We should not be trying to please men to get what we want in life. Instead, we should honor God. In living your life to honor God, you will have better success than you could ever plan, by doing things for self or for men to notice you.

Trust the Lord for the success of your life because it is only what you do for Christ in life, that will last!

God bless you! Have a great day!

Rev Janis Barnes

1. Name at least two to three actions you have participated in that you thought were for the eternal gain and glory of God?

2. What are two to three things you could commit to that are for your eternal gain and glory to God?

3. What will you do to monitor your actions that are consistent with staying on the course of providing glory to God? (Some examples could be prayer, fasting, studying the scripture, council, mentorship etc.).

Email 4

God is Protecting you!

Do not be afraid of the king of Babylon, whom you are now fearing; do not be afraid of him,' declares the LORD, 'for I am with you to save you and deliver you from his hand. (Jeremiah 42:11 NASB)

Good Day!

Have you ever been in a situation where you felt there was no way out? Maybe you felt trapped in a situation and there was someone over you that had authority and had the upper hand over your situation.

In Jeremiah 42:11 the people were afraid and felt trapped under the hand of the King. In Jeremiah 1:19 we are reminded that even when the enemy fights against us, God is with us!

They will fight against you, but they will not overcome you, for I am with you to deliver you," declares the LORD. Therefore, no matter how trapped you feel in a situation, just know that God has the upper hand, and He will deliver you! Trust in the Lord, allow Him to order your steps and:

He will make a **way**!

Rev Janis Barnes

1. In what ways does fear make you feel entrapped in some areas with seemingly no way out?
2. If you did not have these fears, what would you be able to accomplish or overcome?

3. "Fear not" is one of the most repeated commands documented in the Bible. Every time God prepared His people or sent an angel to encourage someone the declaration would always be "Fear Not". How can you use scriptures to help you overcome fear and entrapment?

4. What actions and steps can you take to become fearless in a situation where fear would normally strike your heart? The Lord has confirmed to me in a dream that fear is a spiritual battle. II *Timothy 1:7 Declares God has not given us a spirit of fear but of power, love and of sound mind.* We must yield to God and seek Him so that we can dominate fear so that it no longer dominates us.

Email 5

God knows me!

"Before I formed you in the womb, I knew you, and before you were born, I consecrated you;
I have appointed you a prophet to the nations." (Jeremiah 1:5 NASB)

Good Day!

Isn't it wonderful to know that God knows you? Many people want to be known by people at work, at school, in politics and in church. Many people want to be famous and known by everyone all over the world. However, because God knows me, I'm excited today!

Jeremiah felt like he was not equipped to do what God wanted him to do. God may have called you to do something, yet like Jeremiah, you don't know how you will do it. You are apprehensive about whether you can handle the task.

But, like Jeremiah, God is reminding you that He knows you, and before you were formed in your mother's womb, He consecrated you and equipped you to do what He has called you to do! Allow God to prepare you and in His time, you will do what God has called you to do!

Have a great day!
Rev Janis Barnes

1. Names two experiences in your life that questioned your purpose, and how you viewed God's value of you?

2. How can meditating, reciting and declaring Jeremiah 1:5, change how you view the value of your worth and how you perceive your value and worth to God.

3. Now that you have taken some time to meditate on Jeremiah 1:5 , share how you view your worth and how you believe God views you?

4. How will you overcome (based on Jeremiah 1:5 and at least one other scripture) obstacles that challenge your self-perception and God's perception of you?

Email 6

All my hope is in the Lord

The Lord is my portion, saith my soul; therefore, will I hope in Him. (Lamentations 3:24 KJV)

Good Morning!

Has God ever told you to do something, but no one else understood why you were doing it? You allowed the Lord to order your steps and you trusted Him, your hope was in Him.

My hope is in the Lord, I am walking in faith today, loving and trusting in Him. He promised and showed me that this year is the year of miracles. He showed me He would answer prayers that were prayed and forgotten. He will do things in your life that you have never expected!

My heart is rejoicing today because God is true to His promises! He does answer prayer! Trust Him, believe in Him, put your hope in Him and watch Him do great things!

Have a Great Day!

Rev Janis Barnes

1. As God continues to speak to you, directing you to act on situations beyond your understanding, what scripture, in addition today's scripture can help you fortify your trust in His voice?

2. Meditate on Isaiah 55:8-9. After meditating on this scripture how can you apply this to your faith and your ability to trust God more?

3. How will meditating on Isaiah 55:8-9 build your patience for those promises and miracles that appear to be taking longer than expected?

4. How will you continue to rejoice in all things and what does that mean or look like to you?

Email 7

Be not afraid, only believe!

As soon as Jesus heard the word that was spoken, He saith unto the ruler of the synagogue, Be not afraid, only believe. (Mark 5:36 KJV)

Good Morning!

Have you ever had someone speak negative about something or someone in your life? All they spoke was doom and gloom.

The synagogue ruler in Mark 5:36 went to Jesus and before he could tell Jesus what his problem was; someone said to him why are you bothering Jesus your daughter is already dead.

When people speak negative things into your life, you should be like this ruler and take your situation to Jesus anyway. Don't allow people to speak death into your life. Trust in the Lord, and not in what others speak over your life!

While they are speaking death, God can be blessing you and speak life into your situation! Your "friends" will tell you to get a divorce, when God can bring peace and new life into your marriage!

Have a Great Day!

Rev Janis Barnes

1. Proverbs 18:21 states there is power of life and death in the tongue. Next time you are faced with an encounter similar to the synagogue ruler and you have taken it to Jesus, or you are waiting on the Lord to show up, how will you respond to the naysayer?

2. How will you respond to or speak to your situation in order to reverse the words of the naysayer?

3. It is imperative we speak quickly to our situation by counteracting the death someone attempts to give it by speaking life.

4. What two or more scriptures can you meditate on that will equip you when encountering this type of situation from the above questions?

Have a worry- free day!

Email 8

Rejoice!

Rejoice in the Lord always: and again, I say, Rejoice. (Philippians 4:4 KJV)

Good Morning!

Yes, God can speak through people in your life, nevertheless, Be careful when you listen to others, listen to the Lord first! Be not afraid, only believe!

No matter what you may be going through in life, there is always a reason to Praise the Lord!

Think about where God has brought you from! Think about what He is doing right now!
Even in the midst of the storm, God is still blessing you!

Rejoice and give God the Praise today!

1. **When hurtful experiences and challenges attempt to erase your memories of the monument of the blessings of God how will you rejoice?**

2. **Name a few ways God has brought you through and where He has brought you from?**

3. What will your routine be in order to remember everything from the questions above when your faith is tested?

   Have a Blessed day!
   Rev Janis Barnes

Email 9

God's Plan!

"I know the plans I have for you," announces the Lord. "I want you to enjoy success. I do not plan to harm you. I will give you hope for the years to come. (Jeremiah 29:11 NIRV)

Good Day!

God wants the best for His children. We, so many times worry about, various aspects of our lives, although God promises never to leave us nor forsake us. He promises to provide all our needs according to His riches in glory.

In Jeremiah 29:11 He reminds us yet again, that His plan is to prosper us, give us success and not to harm us, and to give us hope and peace!

Instead of worrying, trust God's Plan!

Rev. Janis Barnes

1. Why has it been so easy to worry than it is to remember God's presence and promises?

2. How can reading God's word daily help you remember that His promises and plan for your life will be fulfilled?

3. How can worship reassure you that He is always near?

4. What will take place when you worship and when you are reading God's word on a daily basis?

Email 10

Bless You!

May the grace of the Lord Jesus Christ be with your spirit. (Philemon 1:25 NIRV)

Good Morning!

It is easy to want nice things for the people that you love or care for. When we pray, besides praying for ourselves, we pray for our families, friends, those people that make a difference in our lives.

In this epistle Paul was writing to his friends and in it, he offered a blessing, a prayer upon them. I began thinking how powerful it is to also bless them that curse you, as Jesus said.

Yes, it is hard to bless someone or pray for someone who does not treat us the same way. Pray for your Boss who doesn't know the Lord, pray for your neighbor who is anything but friendly, pray for your family member that you don't get along with. Pray for that church member who is treating you horribly. Pray for your friend that isn't acting like your friend anymore. Bless them and watch how God will bless you!

Have a Great Day!

Rev Janis Barnes

1. Why may it be much easier to pray for family and loved ones than it would be an enemy or difficult person?

2. How can meditating on Philemon 1:25 provide a strong grace and deposit into your spirit to pray for your enemies?

3. We not only need to pray the blessings for their material well-being but for the well-being of their soul above all things because God wishes none would perish. How can the prayer below help them?

"Father God in the name of Jesus I pray for my enemies that curse me. I do not curse them back but bless them and pray that they get right with God before it's too late".

4. Take the challenge of praying for an enemy or someone who wronged you for a week. **Share how God blessed you after the week was over**

Bless you and have a great day!
Rev Janis Barnes

Email 11

God's Favor!
May the Lord our God show us His favor.
Lord, make what we do succeed.
Please make what we do succeed. (Psalm 90:17 NIRV)
Good Morning!

Have you ever been in situations where no matter what others tried to do to you, it did not succeed? They tried to hold you back, but they couldn't. The Lord always made a way for you! You have experienced God's favor!
Continue to serve Him, continue to put God first in your life. Trust in Him and believe in Him. Watch things turn out right for you. You have God's favor. Let them try to block you, they can't.
They can do only what God allows them to do. Hold on be strong, you have God's favor on your life!
Have a fantastic weekend!

Rev. Janis Barnes

1. Describe in a few words what favor means to you?

2. How have you seen the favor of God, which is His unmerited and undeserved influence at work in a few experiences in your life?

3. Favor is controlled by God's power and jurisdiction. How is God's favor different from man's favor? Do you think God's favor and man's favor were ever both at work in your life?

God's favor is like Him opening a door no man can shut

(Revelation 3:7). What doors has He opened in your life that

no man has been able to shut?

Email 12

Take your burdens to the Lord and leave them there!

Turn your worries over to the Lord.
He will keep you going.
He will never let godly people fall. (Psalm 55:22 NIRV)

Good Morning!

It is so wonderful when God does things in your life, that only He can do. Like, when He orchestrates you meeting or seeing someone that you least expect. Like when you have a bill that's overdue and the Lord makes a way for that bill to be paid and you had no source of income at the time to pay it! Glory to God!

Sometimes we don't always recognize that God is in the midst of our situations, because we are focused on the situations, that we often miss seeing Him at work in the midst. The psalmist in Psalm 55:22 speaks to taking your cares, your worries to the Lord, and He will keep you. He won't let the righteous fall!

In other words, God has you, don't worry! Trust Him! Take your burdens to the Lord and leave them there!

Have a great day!
Rev Janis Barnes

1. Meditate on Psalm 55:22. After meditating, share how you can use that scripture in at least two ways regarding your current situation?

2. As you face current and future trials, ask God to show how He is at work behind the scenes amidst the trial and praise Him in advance! How will this influence the process of the situation?

3. Find a scripture (including the two above) that can shift your thoughts from the problem to the promise?

Email 13

Lord help me do the work!

All of them were trying to frighten us. They thought, "Their hands will get too weak to do the work. So it won't be completed."
 But I prayed to God. I said, "Make my hands stronger." (Nehemiah 6:9 NIRV)
Good Day!
Have you ever been working on something and got some type of opposition? Something or someone tried to block you. But, what's really bad is that you began to believe you couldn't do it!

Nehemiah's enemies tried to block him from doing the work God had charged him to do Nehemiah prayed and asked God to make his hands stronger, so that he could complete the work.
 What do you need strengthened, to get the work done in your life? Ask God today for strength and believe, right now that it's done!
 Have a wonderful day!

Rev Janis Barnes

1. When God gives you instructions for your promise and naysayers and discouragement begin to surface, how can Nehemiah 6:9 assist you in completing the work

2. How can praising the Lords daily in advance be a weapon against opposition?

3. How can discovering your potential that God sees and God's power to deliver you and impact the way you handle opposition in the future according to Numbers 23:19?

4. Find three scriptures about promise. Create three questions for God as to how those promise scriptures apply directly to your calling?

Email 14

Where's the fruit?

"I am the vine. You are the branches. If anyone remains joined to me, and I to him, he will bear a lot of fruit. You can't do anything without me. (John 15:5 NIRV)
Good Morning!

Do you remember the TV commercial where the person asked the question "where's the beef?" I remember how funny it was referring to it as it was not real meat in the sandwich.

As Christians we are to be disciples and witnesses for Christ. We are to spread the good news. Not just by what we say, but by what we do and how we live. Our lives in Christ should be fruitful. We should be real, not just Christians on Sundays or while we are at the church building, but all day every day!

So, I ask the question today, where's the fruit?

Have a fantastic day!

Rev Janis Barnes

1. What is your definition of a fruit inspector?

2. If someone from work/business, church or family would inspect your fruit what would they find?

3. Is it fair for people to judge your words only and not your actions? Explain.

Email 15

It's Possible!

Jesus looked at them and said, "With man, that is impossible. But not with God. All things are possible with God." (Mark 10:27 NIRV)

Good Morning!

What are you facing in your life today? Many people are facing challenges in their lives. Challenges that seem impossible to overcome. You get tired of hearing "no". Who is telling you "no"?

When you look and focus in the natural, things seem impossible to achieve. Jesus said in Mark 10:27:

"With man, that is impossible, But not with God. All things are possible with God."

So today take another look at the situation. This time look in the supernatural, look with the spiritual eye. Look to the Lord, and you will begin to see that:

"It's Possible"! You can make it. You can achieve it. It's there for you. The "no", will become "yes"!
 Yes Lord!

Have an awesome day!

Rev Janis Barnes

1. How does praying on a daily basis help you to become sensitive to how that which is impossible with man is possible with God?

2. How can fasting on a regular basis help you to be sensitive to what is possible with God and impossible with man?

3. What scripture(s), in addition to the ones in this devotional passage (Day 15), can strengthen you to build your faith to believe that at all times, with God all things are possible?

4. Can you share a time you experienced something to be impossible with man, but was possible with God?

Email 16

Your Joy!

Give me back the joy that comes from being saved by you. Give me a spirit that obeys you. That will keep me going. (Psalm 51:12 NIRV)

Good Morning!

Truly the joy of the Lord is my strength. Isn't it something, how when you want to cry, the Lord gives you peace that surpasses understanding. When you think that you can't make it, somehow The Lord makes a way!

King David knew that without the Lord he was nothing. He knew that he slew the giant and many armies because his strength was in the Lord. He also knew real joy is from the Lord.

On this Memorial Day weekend as you remember your loved ones, remember your joy, your strength is from the Lord!

God bless you!

Rev Janis Barnes

1. The enemy knows the joy of the Lord is your strength, so he tries to contend with and drain that joy. How can God restore the joy of your salvation?

2. What daily activities can help you stay fortified with the joy of the Lord? What will you do to ensure you are consistent with those activities?

3. How important is your joy? What can you accomplish with consistent joy that you can't accomplish without it?

Email 17

God will lift you!

Humble yourselves before the Lord, and He will lift you up. (James 4:10 GNT)

Good Morning!

Sometimes it's not easy being a Christian. For me it's not easy, when you want to say something, and God tells you to be quiet, be still. Yet you know you have to be obedient, because you don't know God's full plan, but you know His plan is best.

However, it's awesome when God reveals why He told you to be quiet, or why He told you to do something you didn't understand!

Being humble comes from within and God gives that spirit to you. It's really hard to see others move ahead when you see straight through them and know they are not completely honest. Yet God tells you to be still, be quiet.

Listen to God, humble yourself before God, He will lift you; He will elevate you, not man.
Hold on, be strong, it's not easy being a Christian, but it's worth it!

Have a great day!

Rev Janis Barnes

1. Is God protecting you from the unknown and building your faith in Him when He tells you to be still? What unseen thing could He be shielding you from when He tells you to be quite in the midst of the unknown?

2. Is God trying to quiet the restlessness in your spirit, from the unknown so He can speak to you in an unfamiliar way or by of the Holy Spirit? Explain?

3. Meditate on Romans 8:18 and James 4:10. Does that help build your faith in God and trust Him when you do not understand His plan? If so, explain how?

Have a Great Day!

Rev Janis Barnes

Email 18

Wonderful Revelations!

Call to me, and I will answer you; I will tell you wonderful and marvelous things that you know nothing about. (Jeremiah 33:3 GNT)

Good Morning!

It is wonderful to be in a good relationship. A relationship where you can talk and learn and grow. A relationship where real communication takes place. When your voice is heard and together nothing can stop you.

In Jeremiah 33:3 God spoke again to His people through Jeremiah. And although Jeremiah was confined in prison during that time, it did not stop God's voice to be heard.

Today, no matter what your condition is, your condition or situation cannot stop the great and wonderful, revelation that God has for you. If you call Him, He promises to answer!

He will tell you wonderful things that you don't know! Call on Him today and believe and trust that a renewal will take place in your life!

Have a super day!

Rev Janis Barnes

1. Have you ever called on the Lord and He answered right away? Did it build your faith?
2. Have you ever called on the Lord, but the answer took much longer than you expected? Did God revel to you the reason He had you wait?
3. Were you grateful the answer took longer than expected? What was He protecting you from?
4. Meditate on the devotional scripture of the day. Ask God to prepare and mature you for those great and mighty things you know not so you will be able to receive and maintain the revelation. How will this prepare you for your destiny?

Email 19
The Lord is faithful!

But the Lord is faithful, and He will strengthen you and keep you safe from the Evil One. (II Thessalonians 3:3 GNT)

Good Morning!
Isn't it wonderful to know that you can trust the Lord, no matter what comes? Sometimes you put your faith, hope and trust in people and because people are not perfect, sometimes they fail you.

But the Lord is faithful! He is with you always.

In *II Thessalonians 3:3 it also says He will strengthen you. That's good news*! Not only is He faithful, but He also gives you strength and then He keeps the evil one from you! I am shouting!
God is so true to His promises! Just reading this verse lets us know we can rest safely in the arms of the Lord.

Have a triumphant day!

Rev Janis Barnes

1. Why do you think it is easier at times to choose to trust man, or people instead of God?

2. What can we do daily to help build our trust in God first?

3. How has trusting God strengthened and protected you?

4. Write down ways God has been faithful to you when you trusted Him, and not man. How will this help you if you keep this principle close daily?

Email 20

Grace and Peace!

May God our Father and the Lord Jesus Christ give you grace and peace. (II Thessalonians 1:2 GNT)

Good Morning!

In II Thessalonians 1:2 we see in the salutation of this epistle, Paul writes to the people of that church, to have both God's grace and peace. What a great combination to have! In studying this verse, it was a salutation which blessed the people with God's grace and peace. His grace was referred to as God's favor.

So, on today I greet you with God's grace, His favor upon your life, and with His peace, to calm your fears and give you clear understanding!

God bless you! Have a victorious day!

Rev. Janis Barnes

1. What are some things you have noticed that cause you to run out of grace?
2. How can praying daily and fasting at least one day a week keep you surrounded by God's grace?
3. What are some things that cause you to lose your peace?
4. What Boundaries can you set to ensure your peace prevails?

Email 21

My Shelter!
The Lord is my shepherd; I shall not want. (Psalm 23:1 KJV)
Good Morning!

My Mom asked me an interesting question this morning. I told her I believed the Lord has led me to the house He has for my children and I (and her too, I'm still praying that she will change her mind), here in Dallas, and she said " does it have a shelter?" I wasn't sure if I heard the question correctly, so I asked her "a shelter?" She said, "yes a shelter, in case of storms". I said, "no I didn't see any shelters anywhere."

I began to think, we don't have shelters in Maryland, and we have had bad storms too. I also thought, the Lord is my shelter. He protects me through the storms of life, He is my Jehovah Jireh, my provider! He is my keeper. He is my all and all. In the 23 Psalm, David describes God as our Shepherd. The Shepherd protects His sheep. We are the sheep and God protects us from the wolves we don't see in our lives. When we are lost, He helps us find our way back to the pasture.

Yes, the Lord is my shelter!

Have a fantastic weekend!
Rev. Janis Barnes

1. Reflect on the times you felt insecure and ask God for His shelter of piece to invade your life and soul where you still feel you need His covering. How will this boost your self-esteem and confidence, individually and in Him?

2. When the storms of life rage throughout your journey, how can the scripture reference Psalm 23 secure you in His firm foundation?

3. How has the Lord been a shelter in your life? Share at least three accounts?

4. How has the Lord showing up as a shelter impacted your relationship with Him?

Email 22

Praise God for your Victory!

Then we will shout for joy over your victory and celebrate your triumph by praising to our God.
May the LORD answer all your requests. (Psalm 20:5 GNT)

Good Morning!

One of my best friends is a person who really rejoices and celebrates other people's blessings. This man is genuinely happy when other people have success and their prayers have been answered.

In the 20th Psalm, according to the Matthew Henry Commentary, is a prayer for the Kings of Israel but with relation to Christ.

We should learn to pray for one another. Maybe it is easy to pray for the people we love, but try praying for people that don't like us, we may not necessarily get along with, is not easy!

In Luke 6:28 Jesus tells us: Bless them that curse you, pray for them which despitefully use you.

Today, let's ask the Lord to help us pray for those who make our lives hard. Let's pray and just like my friend, then we will see how God blesses us, because of the love we have shown to others.

Have a victorious day!

Rev. Janis Barnes

1. **Praying for others is a sign of humility to God, especially those who are not so kind to us. How can this also free us up from any resentment and bitterness toward those who wronged us?**

2. **Do you believe doing so will place the focus on your relationship with God as opposed to being consumed by the wrong attitudes some have? Explain.**

3. **Praying for others does not mean you agree with their behavior but that their actions will not overpower you or the will of God. Try doing so to someone you know. How will this keep you free?**

Email 23

God has not forgotten you!

I am weak and poor, O Lord, but you have not forgotten me. You are my savior and my God—hurry to my aid! (Psalm 40:17 GNT)

Good Morning!
The song by Tonex is ringing in my spirit today; "God has not forgot. " In the song the lyrics say: "If He said that He would do it, it will come to past. God has not forgot." Just keep on believing God has not forgot .....

Many of us like the Psalmist in Psalm 40 and the singer Tonex, know that God has not forgotten us. However, when you are going through tests and trials of life, sometimes, do you ask God has He forgotten you or does He see, what you are going through? Sometimes it seems like the enemy just won't let up!

But I decree and declare this morning, that God has not forgotten you! He will help you! He will, and He is coming to aid you, He will carry you through! You will get through this!

That set back, that disappointment, is only temporary. God is working behind the scenes, working out a miracle for you! Start praising Him today, what you've been looking for will be better than what you asked for!

God has not forgotten you!

God bless you abundantly!

Rev Janis Barnes

1.Why is it so easy to believe God has forgotten us?

2.Share some testimonies of how God showed up when you thought He had forgotten you?

3.How can praying and meditating on God's word daily and abiding in His spirit daily remove any thoughts that God has forgotten you?

4.How can thanking and praising God daily regardless of the circumstances increase your remembrance of His faithfulness?

Email 24

What Will God require?

He hath shewed thee, O man, what is good; and what doth the Lord require of thee, but to do justly, and to love mercy, and to walk humbly with thy God? (Micah 6:8 KJV)

Good morning!

Have you ever thought about what God requires of us? There are so many rules and regulations that man has but what does God say?

In Micah 6:8 we see that God requires us to be just, to do what's right, to be kind and to walk humbly with God to serve Him. If we are walking with Him then we should know Him, be in a relationship with Him.

Today Lord I pray that You always lead us to do the right thing, in our lives, be kind to others and to ourselves and to have a close, real relationship with You and that we stay humble before you. In Jesus' name we pray Amen!

Have an Awesome day!
Rev. Janis Barnes

1.Does God requires a pure heart above all else?

2.How can you allow Him to heal and purify your heart?

3.How can opening your heart to God open up your spirit to Him to hear exactly what he requires of you?

4.What can you do to open your heart to God?

Email 25
Don't worry God will provide!
Instead, be concerned above everything else with the Kingdom of God and with what He requires of you, and He will provide you with all these other things. (Matthew 6:33 GNT)

Good Morning!

It's hard to think sometimes when you have a lot on your mind. There are so many thoughts at one time, it seems like you can't focus on one thing. People are wondering how their bills will be paid. Is the job they have enough or when will they get a job? People are concerned if their health will hold up? With all the decisions to make in life and with life constantly changing, no wonder people begin to worry.

Jesus said in Matthew the 6th chapter that God clothes the lilies of the field, and he takes care of the little sparrow; surely, He will provide for us! In the 33rd verse He says that we should seek and focus on the Kingdom of God, and all the things that we worry about, He will provide!

Trust the Lord today, focus on Him, He will provide!
 Have a beautiful day!
Rev. Janis Barnes

1.How can prayer and worship clear our mind?

2.How can studying the word allow our minds to stay on the Lord regardless of what tries to compete for your attention?

3.How can casting down all imagination that opposes God help you when thoughts come to bombard you?

4. When we cast down the thoughts that are not of God and only accept those that are of God how will this change the trajectory of our day and our outlook on our situation?

Email 26

Positive Attitude!

Give at least two warnings to those who cause divisions, and then have nothing more to do with them. (Titus 3:10 GNT)

Good morning!
Have you ever been around someone who never has anything pleasant to say? They are mad with everything and everybody. They think everybody is out to get them, and they try to convince you that people are out to get you as well?

In Titus, an epistle or letter written by Paul to Titus, gives instructions to the church leaders. We see in Titus 3:10 it says,

Give at least two warnings to those who cause divisions, and then have nothing more to do with them.

We can apply this teaching to our lives. When people constantly stir up trouble and cause division, it may be hard, but sometimes you have to walk away.

Surround yourself with people who help you grow, not hinder you, who have a positive attitude. If you have a hard time with this begin to pray today to ask God to help you with this. Pray for those who constantly have a negative attitude, ask God to give them peace.

Have a wonderful weekend!
Rev Janis Barnes

1. How can failure to set boundaries with those that stir up strife compromise your witness and your ability to avoid being pessimistic?

2. Do you have a hard time telling even the most difficult person no?

3. How can failure to say no to someone have a negative impact on your peace and destiny?

4. How can prayer assist you with not compromising and setting boundaries with toxic people and situations?

Email 27

The Truth!

See to it that no one takes you captive through hollow and deceptive philosophy, which depends on human tradition and the elemental spiritual forces of this world rather than on Christ. (Colossians 2:8 NIV)

Good morning!

You know when you are being effective for Christ when the enemy attacks you with full force. It was a Saturday, and I was leaving out of a parking lot (driving), when I saw a woman entering the parking lot. I motioned to give her the right-away, I was being courteous. This woman cursed me out, with children in the car saying you need to drive.... I couldn't believe it!

Then later still the same day, just as night was falling, as I went into the Chinese restaurant with my youngest son, two gentlemen approached me dressed in Old Testament garments. I have seen them many times in different locations of the city, at night-time. I even researched them because a friend that I grew up with in church is now a part of this group.

One of the gentlemen offered me a paper, I told him no thank you. He said "you don't want to know about your salvation? About the truth, who you are?" I told him " I know about my salvation; I know the truth Praise the Lord." He says as he is walking away "no you don't ", I said with a smile "yes, yes I do."

We see in Colossians that Paul is reminding the church, not to be deceived, by false teachings.

We are living in the last days; no man knows when the Lord will come back for the church. But I do know the enemy is running scared and there are false doctrines being taught now more than ever. Keep yourselves rooted and grounded in the word!

Lord, I pray today for your children, God continue to cover us from the enemy, continue to allow us to be your light in the darkness. We pray for people who are falling for these false doctrines and teachings, God let them hear the truth and accept you before it's too late. In Jesus' name we pray amen!

Have a victorious day!
Rev. Janis Barnes

1.Test and trials will come and opposition, which are distractions from the enemy. What power has God given you to counteract these tests and opposition?

2. Meditate on Ephesians Chapter 6. How can this assist you in understanding how to engage opposition?

3. How can you assure that you will pass the tests when you are tested?

4. How can you keep a positive attitude despite opposition?

Email 28

No greater love!

I pray that out of His glorious riches He may strengthen you with power through His Spirit in your inner being, so that Christ may dwell in your hearts through faith. And I pray that you, being rooted and established in love, may have power, together with all the Lord's holy people, to grasp how wide and long and high and deep is the love of Christ, and to know this love that surpasses knowledge—that you may be filled to the measure of all the fullness of God. (Ephesians 3:16-19 NIV)

Good Morning!

If you were to convey one word to people who are not saved, to explain the gospel what word would you give? The word that I would give is love.

In Ephesians 3:16-19 today, Paul wrote to the church of Ephesus, I am writing to you. That in everything that we do for the church, it should all be about building the Kingdom of God, it should all be about the love that God has for us. When you think about the love, you can make it through anything.

My prayer today is that we truly experience the Love of God. When you are going through, stop, breathe and think about how much the Lord loves you. Enough to come to dwell on earth, to take on our sins, to die for us. To be resurrected, to leave a comforter, to dwell in us, and the promise to come back for us! My prayer is also for those who don't know Christ, for God to open their hearts and mind to His love today.

There is no greater love!
Have a wonderful day!
Reverend Janis Barnes

1. What is your definition of the word extravagant? Have you experienced the extravagant love of the father? Explain.

2. How can meditating on the scripture reference place you in a position to experience the greater love of the father?

3. How can you testify in your personal life of no greater love anyone else has for you but the Lord?

4. Do you believe His love fights for you? How so?

Email 29
Man meant it for evil, but God meant it for your good!

You intended to harm me, but God intended it for good to accomplish what is now being done, the saving of many lives. (Genesis 50:20 NIV)

Good morning!

When I read this passage of scripture, it reminded me of the saying "Man meant it for evil, but God meant it for good." Implying that someone tried to cause something bad to happen to you, but God used it to bless you!

In this scripture Joseph was talking to his brothers after their father Jacob had died. His brothers became worried that Joseph would take revenge on them, for what they had done to him. So, his brothers sent word to Joseph saying it was what their father said; forgive your brothers for the sins and the wrongs they have done to you. However, Joseph did not have any malice in his heart towards them. Joseph replied to his brothers:
You intended to harm me, but God intended it for good to accomplish what is now being done, the saving of many lives (Genesis 50:20 NIV).

There are so many lessons we can learn from Joseph. One is true forgiveness. My prayer is that today we can truly forgive, with no malice in our hearts. Remembering that we don't have to avenge people for what they have done, because God says vengeance is mine.

**What man meant for evil, God meant it for good!
Have an awesome day in the Lord!
Have a Great Day!**

Rev Janis Barnes

1. How can unforgiveness block your favor or prayers?

2. Do you believe that some people desire to forgive but cannot seem to?

3. How can understanding the process of forgiveness provide sweet liberty?

4. Praying and fasting can break the chains of unforgiveness. How can this freedom bring you closer to the father and your destiny?

Email 30
No one can stop God's plan for you!

"I know that You can do all things;
no purpose of Yours can be thwarted. (Job 42:2 NIV)

Good Morning!

It is a good morning! I'm grateful because the Lord woke me up this morning and has blessed my family and I beyond measure. Just to look back over my life, even when I was not obedient and didn't wait on God, Him, He still blessed me and is still fulfilling His purpose and His plan in my life! Hallelujah!

You may feel that it is too late for God to still fulfill His purpose in your life. You may think that you have been wasting years and you still don't know what your purpose is? You may think you are not where God wants you to be. You may feel that someone is holding you back.
 God wants you to know today, No one can block or stop God's purpose or plan for you! Not even you!

Lord, I come today praying for you to move today on your children's lives, God, someone is frustrated because they have been waiting and asking, "what do you want me to do, for you Lord"? They have been struggling with what their purpose is. What plan do You have for their life? God, please speak to them, and make it plain. Lord we are praying " take my life and let it be consecrated Lord to thee ....." Thank you, Lord, in advance for what you are about to do! In Jesus' name Amen!

God bless you! Have a magnificent day!
Rev Janis Barnes

1. Meditate and confess Job 42:2 daily. How can this assist you in dominating discouragement and opposition?

2. How does thankfulness shut the mouth of the enemy?

3. How can the prayer above cause you to rise above tests and opposition?

Email 31
I know the Lord for myself!

My ears had heard of You but now my eyes have seen You. (Job 42:5 NIV)
Good morning!

Many of us as children growing up, our parents took us to Sunday school or to church or you heard someone talk about the Lord or on Sundays you heard hymns being played.

Somehow, you heard about God. Maybe you didn't hear about Him until you were a teenager or older, but you heard about Him. I am rejoicing today like Job in the verse shared today, Job said: My ears had heard of you but now my eyes have seen you. (Job 42:5 NIV)

It is something about seeing the Lord and knowing Him for yourself! Having a personal relationship with Him is awesome, and there is nothing like it! I am glad to say today, that I know the Lord for myself!

Lord, thank you for allowing me to know you. Lord there are still many who don't know you. I come today interceding on their behalf, Lord, speak to their hearts and let them hear you. Use your children that do know you, to be a light, so that they may see you, in us. In Jesus' name Amen!

Have a fantastic weekend!
Rev Janis Barnes

1. What is your first memory of experiencing God and truly knowing Him and not simply hearing about Him?

2. Share three things that you can say about your relationship with God?

3. How much time do you invest with your relationship with God?

4. How would ten extra minutes in the morning and night spent with God strengthen your relationship with Him?

Email 32
I'm so glad God's ways are not our ways!

"For my thoughts are not your thoughts, neither are your ways my ways," declares the Lord. (Isaiah 55:8 NIV)

Good Morning!

When you think about our justice system in theory it is supposed to be, "innocent until proven guilty". But that is not always the case for all people.
It seems like, it is in our nature to judge people or situations before we know all the facts. Some people don't want to know the facts, they just jump to conclusions or listen to what other people think.

I'm so glad God is not so quick to judge us the way, people do. Some are quick to judge based simply on what a person's thought or perception is of someone, that's it. Many people are ready to fight, because someone just looked at them, both children and adults.

I'm so glad that God loves us unconditionally, with no strings attached. God loves when we grow, and He doesn't hinder or stifle our growth. I'm so glad God's ways are not our ways, and His thoughts are not our thoughts.
You may be in a situation that you think there is no good solution, just remember, God's ways are not our ways! He can change the situation in a way we would never have thought.

Don't give up, it's not over!

Have a marvelous day!
Rev Janis Barnes

1. Being judgmental can stem from one's upbringing or circle of influence or how they were judged. What ways have you been automatically judgmental?

2. How can you rethink your judgmental tendencies and allow grace to people or the situation you are judging?

3. The Bible says judge not lest we be judged. Have you ever judged someone for the same thing you did or were doing?

4. How does having mercy or being slow to judge allow mercy and favor for you?

Email 33
Believe!

"If you can?" said Jesus. "Everything is possible for one who believes." (Mark 9:23 NIV)

Good Morning!

I love this passage of scripture. Jesus is talking to a Father, about healing his son. Jesus asks the man how long has his son been like that? The man says since childhood. Then the man says, if you can do anything, take pity on us, and help us. Jesus replies:
"'If you can'?" said Jesus. "Everything is possible for one who believes." (Mark 9:23 NIV)

I like that "If you can?" The word "if" just stands out. It was almost like Jesus was saying, do you know who I am? "If you can?" Really! Then He says anything is possible for the one who believes.
We are still saying the same thing to Jesus today "If you can" If you would "... Jesus wants us to have no doubts about what He can do, just believe. He wants us to have childlike faith, children believe their parents can do anything, when they are very young.

Lord, help us today to have no doubts, when we come to you. Lord, forgive us. Some of us have trust issues and even when we come to you, we have trouble believing. Lord, I believe, help my unbelief, in Jesus' name Amen!

Have a stress-free day!
Rev Janis Barnes

1. According to Mark 9:23 there is nothing God cannot do If we believe. Does the delay of the promise mean you lack belief?

2. Delay can happen when God is needing you to walk through the reparation process. What scriptures can keep you optimistic during this time?

3. How does being confident in who you are in God and every promise build your expectation of what you believe?

Email 34
A treasure in my heart

I have hidden your word in my heart that I might not sin against you. Psalm 119:11 NIV

Good morning!

It is wonderful when you have something special that you know about. Something that you know, that when you think about it, makes you smile.

When we study the word of God it should be a life changing agent. Whether you have it in your hand or not, it should be a part of you.

The Psalmist says in the 119 Psalms that the word should be hidden in our heart that we might not sin against God. It is like a treasure, in our hearts, that shines within us. When situations arise in our lives, the Holy Spirit reminds us through that word in our hearts, what to do and what to say. He leads and guides us through the word in our hearts.

I get excited to walk around; knowing that within me is a treasure in my heart!

Have a great day!
Rev Janis Barnes

1. A great way to ensure the word of God continues to make you smile and is indwelling and overflowing in you, is to find two to three of your favorite scriptures. What are some of your favorite scriptures?

2. How can these favorite scriptures assist you during times of tests and temptation?

3. Is sin simply and act or can sin also be a thought? Does Proverbs 23:7 clarify this question? How so?

4. How can meditating on scripture counteract thoughts and temptation to act out sin?

Email 35

You don't have to worry!
I was young and now I am old, yet I have never seen the righteous forsaken or their children begging bread. Psalms 37:25 NIV

Good Morning!

I love Psalms 37:25! When things look like there is no way out it will turn out in my favor, I'm talking about financially especially, God reminds me of this verse.

Donald Lawrence and the Tri City Singers sing a song from this verse, and I love the verse in the lyrics that says, "you don't have to worry about a thing, if you're holy and righteous".

Yes, that is a reminder today. You may be doing a financial juggling act. You may be going through difficulties at work, at home, with your family or friends. But you don't have to worry about a thing. God will make a way for you. A door may have closed. Look for another door or window to open for you! It's true, I have never seen the righteous forsaken or their children begging for bread.

Have an outstanding weekend!

Rev Janis Barnes

1. How can meditating on Psalm 37:25 secure you in your mind and heart that you are never forsaken and never have to beg for bread?

2. The Psalms are full of documentation of God's Love for you. Find another scripture in the Psalm similar to Psalm 37:25 reminding you of God's acceptance? What is the scripture?

3. What door has closed for you causing you to be waiting on another?

4. What scripture will you use as your foundation and encouragement for God to bring clarity regarding the door that needs to open and your preparation for when it is time to walk through that door?

Email 36

If it had not been for the Lord on my side, where would I be?
If it had not been for the Lord on my side when men rose against us Psalm 124:2 KJV

Good morning!
When I think about some of the things I have done in my life, some decisions that I made, I know it was the Lord that kept me and protected me! I think about that old hymn of the church "If it had not been for the Lord on my side, where would I be?
In the 124 Psalms the Psalmist declares that very statement. He says:
If the Lord had not been on our side when people attacked us, they would have swallowed us alive Psalms 124:2-3.
How many times have people attacked you nevertheless their plans didn't succeed, but the Lord protected you?
How many times did it seem like you were not going to get out of a situation, but because the Lord was on your side, the favor of the Lord carried you?
I'm so glad the Lord is on my side! I'm so glad to know the Lord Has His hand on me and it is because of Him and His favor I know I can make it!
Give God praise today and remember: if it had not been for the Lord on my side, where would I be?

Have an awesome day!

Rev Janis Barnes

1. When believers make a statement that The Lord is on their side, in your own words, what do you think they truly mean?

2. Can you remember a time or times when the Lord was on your side? What was your confirmation that He was on your side?

3. Can you explain why the Lord remained on your side? Was it prayer? Was it obedience? Or was it just His mercy and grace?

4. What scripture(s) can you find to encourage you when times become challenging that the Lord will have your back?

Email 37

The pursuit of happiness!
Whoever pursues righteousness and love finds life, prosperity and honor. Proverbs 21:21 NIV
Good Morning!

I remember watching the heart felt story of the life of Chris Gardner played by Will Smith. My heart was heavy watching this movie. When Gardner became homeless with his young son, first trying to make it as a salesman then trying to get a break in a stock brokerage as an intern.

The word happiness was spelled right outside of his son's daycare. Many people spend their whole lives trying to be happy. Many people never find true happiness.

In Proverbs 21:21 we see the writer does not say whoever pursues happiness, rather whoever pursues righteousness and love, finds life, prosperity and honor. Matthew 6:33 says "Seek ye first the Kingdom of God and His righteousness and all these things will be added into you ". The Key to both of these verses is to seek God and His righteousness, then happiness, prosperity, honor and life you will find.

God bless you!

Have a tremendous day!

Rev Janis Barnes

1. What did happiness mean or look like to you before your relationship with God?

2. How is the peace, joy, and contentment of God different from happiness?

3. What does seeking God's righteousness mean and how will you pursue His righteousness?

4. Name ways that you put God first and seek His righteousness first as well as ways you can increase putting Him first and seeking His righteousness?

Email 38

Radical Praise!

Why am I discouraged? Why is my heart so sad? I will put my hope in God! I will praise Him again--my Savior and my God! Psalms 42:11 NLT

Good Morning!

What a wonderful day! It is great to wake up and begin giving God the honor, glory and the praise. Our God is worthy to be praised!

However, when you are going through a valley experience, sometimes it's hard to praise God when you don't feel His presence, when your very soul feels dry. The psalmist in Psalms 42:11 says:

Why am I discouraged? Why is my heart so sad? I will put my hope in God! I will praise him again--my Savior and my God!

That's what we have to do, even when we are down and don't feel like praising God, give Him a radical praise and praise Him anyhow. Praise Him in spite of what we feel and what we are going through. Knowing that He is the same God that brought you through before, and He promised never to leave us nor forsake us. Psalms 37:1 says I will bless the Lord at ALL TIMES and His praise will continually be in my mouth!

Give God a Radical Praise today!
God bless you
Rev. Janis Barnes

1. How will praising God confuse the enemy that is trying to discourage or sadden you or break your focus?

2. How can praising God intensify His presence in your life?

3. When you praise God in the midst of adversity how does God respond to your situation?

4. How can praise be protection and invite peace and perseverance when the test or trial is completed?

Email 39

Trust in the Lord!

Trust in the Lord and do good; dwell in the land and enjoy safe pasture.

Take delight in the Lord and He will give you the desires of your heart. Psalm 37:3-4 NIV

Good morning!

We say trust in the Lord, but do we really trust Him?

When we make decisions in our lives do we consult Him? So many times, in our flesh we focus on our problems rather than the problem solver. I'm guilty of that sometimes myself. When we see that, we have to pray and ask the Lord to forgive us for not trusting Him and ask Him to lead us in what we should do.

Have a Great Day!

Rev Janis Barnes

1. What is your definition of trust?

2. What two scriptures can build your foundation of trust when temptation to fear and doubt God, presents itself to trust what you don't see, when you are affected with what you see?

3. How important is your faith when building trust?

4. How can understanding that trust is a process and not a one- day journey assist you on an enduring a hopeful journey, assuring you that the Lord will make a way?

Conclusion

Now that you have completed the devotional journey you can reset and continue the journey daily. You have meditated on the word; you have prayed, and you have grown in many areas where there were struggles to grow and mature. Your confidence in God hopefully has become more rooted and grounded and fashioned into His purpose.

Your perspective may be different on life depending on how you perceive your situations as well as how well you wait in expectation of Him. Above anything else I trust this devotion has certainly convinced you beyond a shadow of a doubt that the Lord with make a way for you!

Rev Janis Barnes

Back of Book/About The Author

Pastor Janis Barnes is the Pastor of Bradford Chapel AME Church in Bonham, Texas. She is a facilitator and a life coach who speaks and ministers to women groups. Her classes and workshops involve activities to bring the content to life! Pastor Barnes is a mother of four and a caregiver for her mother. Pastor Barnes has a Prayer and Devotion Ministry where she prays daily for others and sends scriptures and devotions to many to lift up the name of Jesus. She is a Breast Cancer Survivor! She recently started a Breast Cancer Support Group for Breast Cancer patients, survivors and their families on Facebook called Breast Cancer Survivors. She can be reached at: JanisBarnes28@gmail.com

Pastor Barnes has a Bachelor of Science Degree from Coppin State College. A member of Alpha Kappa Alpha Sorority Inc. She has worked for 7 Eleven Inc for 22 years this July, 2023 At 7 - Eleven she has been a Certified Business Consultant, Zone Merchandiser for Fresh Food and a Corporate Learning Facilitator. Currently, she is in Field Operations as a Fresh Food Field Program Coach. More than anything Pastor Barnes loves the Lord and is grateful for all that He has done for her and her family!

www.ingramcontent.com/pod-product-compliance
Lightning Source LLC
Chambersburg PA
CBHW070550090426
42735CB00013B/3134